WHEN GOD DOESN'T SHOW UP ON TIME

HOW TO DEAL WITH UNEXPECTED OUTCOMES

MIRIAM JONES

REALLY**EDUCATED**

REALLY**EDUCATED**

This book is not intended to provide personalized legal, accounting, financial, mental or emotional health, therapy, or investment advice. Readers are encouraged to seek the counsel of competent professionals regarding such matters as interpretation of the law, proper accounting procedures, financial planning, mental health counseling, personal therapy, and investment strategies. The Author and Publisher specifically disclaim any liability, loss, or risk which is incurred as a consequence, directly or indirectly, of the use and application of any of the contents of this work.

www.reallyeducated.com

ISBN: 979-8-9880973-5-8 (Paperback)

979-8-9880973-4-1 (E-book)

This is for the ones in the dark, ready to throw in the towel. This is for true believers who are jaded and tired. It is for those with pain and scars, but hearts of gold and dreams of giants. Hang in there. This is for you.

CONTENTS

ISN'T HE ALWAYS ON TIME?

He may not come when you want Him...we all know the rest of that popular phrase. But how many times have you wished and prayed about a situation, and it just didn't change? How many times have you asked God to take thoughts or struggles away but it hasn't happened? How about standing faithfully, believing that someone would come around, or a problem would clear up, and it falls apart instead?

If you have ever been in any of those positions, then this book is for you.

Life is hard. There is no way around it. Sometimes the challenges that we face can rock us to our core, and having faith becomes a struggle. The bottom line is, that during your weakest moments, it can be difficult to stay focused.

This book will provide insight into ways that you can navigate your dark season with courage. It will also provide practical applications and opportunities for reflection on your circumstances. If you are down and out and looking for what to do, please continue reading because this one is for you.

ONE

GOD WHERE ARE YOU?

How many times have you spoken those words? Quite a few, I bet. It is easy to do, especially when we live in a physical world and have faith based on an invisible source. But the reality is, the hope that we share is made tangible through nature. Step outside and take a moment to look around. What do you see? Clouds, the sun, grass, trees, birds, maybe even a lake. Incredible right? You know what else? That is God.

God is all around us. His spirit is in all creation. Often, we become so distracted with our issues that we forget to embrace the reality of God's presence in the earth.

Observe how the trees go through seasons and survive by adapting to environmental changes. They are specially designed and equipped to do so. Just like the trees, you were created to endure. With the strength of God's spirit, you have everything that you need to face every situation.

Practical Application

For the next seven days, set aside time to embrace nature. Go on a walk and observe your environment. Watch the sunrise or sunset. Sit by the ocean or a lake.

Reflection

How can you appreciate God's presence in your surroundings?

Meditation

God, help me to embrace your love by appreciating your creation.

TWO
I STILL FEEL ALONE

Surrounded by people but still feeling alone? It happens. And when it does, there are a few things to remember. First, you are loved. No matter if you have or do not have family, friends, mentors, coaches, a spouse, pets, or children, it doesn't matter. There is someone who loves you, and in fact, is the very essence of love itself.

Second, let's figure out why you are feeling this way. Is it possible that you have withdrawn because you don't think that anyone will understand? Or maybe you are afraid or ashamed of being judged, or you just don't want to be a burden on anyone else.

All of these are very real feelings. But you know what? It means that you are human, and that's a good thing. The reality is, no one can help you if they don't know that you are hurting. Often, God will use people to answer your prayers. If you are not open to receiving, it can be very difficult to understand this.

Sometimes we try to hide and figure things out on our own. Then we put the pressure on God to perform to our expectations, and when that doesn't happen, we get frustrated and angry. Could it be that He moves differently than we think? We can get so wrapped up in what we believe should be the solution, that we miss the way out because of our own shortsightedness.

Loneliness is the result of disconnection. The solution? Get connected. Open your heart and mind to truly receive guidance and assistance in whatever form God chooses to send it. The highest and most important connection, of course, is to the master.

Practical Application

Every day this week, look in the mirror and say, "I am loved. I am wonderfully made."

Reflection

In what ways can you open yourself up to new connections?

Meditation

God, help me to let go of my expectations and receive what you have for me.

YOU'RE NEVER ALONE

In the midst of the darkness there exists a light. You don't have to fight alone.

THREE
THAT'S NICE BUT MY SITUATION IS NOT CHANGING

Aww.... yes, the waiting period. Perhaps the most difficult part of it all. You have faith, you've read and listened, and you are walking in your belief, but everything is still the same, or worse. It's definitely a hard season to be in. No one can tell you when it will end or exactly why it is happening, so I will not try. However, there is a reason for it, and no matter what that reason is, every day you survive is another day closer to better. It doesn't sound glamorous or exciting, but it is true.

We hope in the glory to come. There is nothing wrong with surrender. There's also nothing wrong with talking to God. The more you communicate, the more opportunity you give Him to show up on your behalf.

Let's see, life isn't fair, and some people are better equipped to face certain situations than others. Despite this, there is nothing that you are going through that someone else hasn't. If they made it, so can you.

Your responsibility is to trust and put yourself in the best possible position to receive deliverance. This is done by looking at the actions that you can take to maintain a positive atmosphere. Keeping your mind in check, keeping your heart pure, surrounding yourself with like-minded individuals who can support you, being a good steward of what you currently have, walking uprightly, and seeking wisdom in decision-making are all ways that you can remain stable while walking through the valley.

Practical Application

For the next seven days, pick one positive quote or scripture to read each morning.

Reflection

What can you do to keep your mind and heart in alignment?

Meditation

God, help me to have the patience to endure.

FOUR
WELL I'M TIRED NOW SO...

There is rest for your soul if you want it. Let go. No one is expected to carry the universe on their shoulders 24/7. You were not made for that. That's God's job.

He says if you come to Him, He will give you rest. What does that mean? It means to stop trying to do everything yourself. It means you can stop trying to hide your struggles in work or distract your mind by taking on additional responsibilities. It means there is nothing wrong with sitting in silence. Nothing wrong with having a good cry.

Nothing wrong with taking a nap. Nothing wrong with shutting off your phone. Nothing wrong with finding a quiet place to reflect. Nothing wrong with not finishing all of your tasks for the day.

There is nothing wrong with being tired and finding rest. God is the Good Shepherd. He will take care of you. He understands that you are trying your best. He understands that you are frustrated. And even when you don't feel like he cares, He does. So just be tired. It is okay.

Practical Application

Dedicate one hour each day this week to relaxing.

Reflection

What additional responsibilities have you taken on that make you feel overwhelmed?

Meditation

God, help me to understand that I don't have to be perfect.

CHANGE IS COMING

What you see now is only temporary. Find peace in knowing that your lack of control is an opportunity for a miracle.

FIVE
I QUIT

Whoa, whoa, whoa! Are you sure that you want to do that? I get it, been there, done that. You know what? It probably isn't worth it. Especially if you truly believe and are just terribly disappointed right now. But should you decide to walk that path, guess what? God still loves you. Literally, you can't get away from it, even if you try. If His spirit is within you, there will be conviction. No matter how much you want to do you, you still will not be satisfied. There will be something missing.

But seriously, this is a critical point in your life. You have faced or are facing a situation that you no longer have control over. Whether your heart has been broken or things just didn't work out the way you expected, it can be crushing.

This is a time when you probably don't want to hear any more scriptures, have any more prayer, see any more positive quotes or encouragement, or even talk to anyone who is in a better position. You're resentful that things did not work out, and that God did not show up on time. Understandable. The decision you make at this point can truly alter the days to come. Before you make an emotional move, take some time to reflect on what it could mean for your future.

Practical Application

For the next seven days, write down the positive and negative impacts that giving up on your faith could have on your life.

Reflection

How did you get to this point?

Meditation

God, help me to make the right decision.

SIX

I CHANGE MY MIND

Because you have made the decision to continue your journey, let's focus on getting you built back up so that you don't end up in this place again. But if you do, there is grace and forgiveness. Compassion and mercy are renewed every single day. So, no worries.

The first step in moving forward is repentance. That means you're making the choice to stop thinking that way and start asking God to renew a right spirit in you. Renew your mind, renew your faith, and renew your heart. If things are going to get better, you've got to open yourself back up and let go of the hurt and anger that got you there. It's no mistake that you're at this place.

Remember at the beginning of the book I said it's all for a reason? Well, the perfecting of your faith is a continuous process. Now that you have endured the pain and struggle of that season, your level of understanding and ability to stand firm have increased. You know things now that you never knew before, and it is time to put that into your tool kit so the next time you encounter a similar season, you will be better equipped to face it.

Practical Application

Take 10 minutes each day this week to write down one thing that you are thankful for.

Reflection

Think about what changes you want to make in your life moving forward.

Meditation

God, help me to live a better life.

EMBRACE THE OPPORTUNITY

A second chance exists by the power of your decision. Open your heart to receive that which is given.

SEVEN

HELP ME GET BACK RIGHT

You walked away, and now you're back. The scars are still fresh, but you're willing to give it another go. What you need now is a little bit of guidance and support. So, the first thing you're going to do is start filling yourself up with the right content on a regular basis. Whether you listen to a podcast, a sermon, or find a verse of the day app, make sure that you are listening to or engaging with scripture daily. It doesn't have to be a long-drawn-out thing. Simply focus on being consistent.

Something else that you can do is begin keeping a journal. Each day, reflect on your feelings and goals, then evaluate your progress. This will help you to develop discipline and process any leftover emotions that you might have.

Next, you guessed it, talk to God. Set aside some time, whether it's first thing in the morning or right before bed. It doesn't have to be complicated; simply thank Him for another day and ask for guidance.

Again, the point is to create a consistent flow of positive input and open communication.

Practical Application

Find a faith-based podcast to listen to each day this week.

Reflection

Think about what your faith really means to you.

Meditation

God, help me to be open to learning and growing.

EIGHT

WHAT ABOUT CHURCH?

Gathering to worship on a regular basis is very important. There is something uplifting about being around others with the same beliefs as you. In fact, that's a major reason why attending service in person is so valuable. It gives you a chance to meet other people who have been in your shoes or are currently where you are. Not only that, but you also never know; you could find yourself helping someone else in the process.

Many organizations even have special small group meetings throughout the week where you can connect and serve. It's basically a built-in community to promote your spiritual growth and relationship with God and others, which is so important.

Right now, you may only be able to attend online or virtually, which is great! But if you get the opportunity, I strongly encourage you to take the chance and attend a live gathering.

Practical Application

Research local congregations in your area and attend at least one service this month.

Reflection

How can engaging with other believers help you in your journey?

Meditation

God, help me to make the right connections.

OPEN YOUR HEART

Be surrounded by the truth to find life's meaning. Virtue is maintained through graceful humility.

NINE

SO, WHAT NOW?

Now that you have established a routine of studying, praying, and making connections on a regular basis, it's time to do some self-improvement. As humans, we are not only spirit and soul but body too. The key to maintaining a healthy life is balance. As you continue to grow stronger in your faith, always remember to increase your capacity in other areas of your life.

This involves learning new things, developing your talents, eating right, exercising, keeping a productive mindset, and walking in your purpose. Each step will become clearer as you make forward progress.

I want to encourage you to **take one day at a time**. It's easy to want to jump right in and be a superhero, but take it slow.

Enjoy each day and cherish the little things. The journey ahead of you will be filled with ups and downs, but you know what? You can make it, just like you have already. I believe in you and know your best is yet to come!

Practical Application

Create a daily schedule that includes time for study, meditation, exercise, learning, and recreation.

Reflection

What is one self-improvement goal that you can accomplish in the next three months?

Meditation

God, help me to walk in total wellness.

TEN

A SPECIAL INVITATION

I hope that you have enjoyed this book. Maybe this is your first time reading about God or hearing things taught like this. Maybe you picked it up out of desperation and in search of answers. One thing I want you to know is that God loves you. If you are looking for a sign, this is it. He sees your heart and knows your situation.

God has a plan for your life. He sent His Son to die for your sins and raised him from the dead so that you could have eternal life. If you believe this and would like to experience all that God has for you, take a moment to ask Him to come into your heart today. It is a free gift, and you are formally invited to receive it.

Practical Application

Take the time right now to ask God to help you live a life in line with His plans for you.

Reflection

Think about how you feel at this moment.

Meditation

Thank you, God, for another chance.

ACKNOWLEDGMENTS

Thanks be to God, the true author and creator of all things beautiful. Special appreciation to everyone who has contributed to this journey of learning, growing, abiding, and enduring. Love flows freely and is embraced totally in return.

ABOUT THE AUTHOR

Miriam Jones is an American author who creates content that helps people learn how to live a life of fulfillment and purpose. Although she holds degrees in marketing and law, Miriam's greatest passion is using her gifts to inspire others to succeed. Her works focus on presenting information in a way that is simple, practical, and encouraging. Readers are challenged to put what they have learned into immediate action, which creates accelerated results.

ALSO BY MIRIAM JONES

How to Live a Happy Life: 7 Keys to Get You Started

Five Steps to Living Your Dream: How to Build Your Life the Right Way